DR. BOB'S
AMAZING WORLD OF
ANIMALS
KOALAS

By Ruth Owen

WINDMILL
BOOKS

New York

Published in 2014 by Windmill Books, An Imprint of Rosen Publishing
29 East 21st Street, New York, NY 10010

Editor for Ruby Tuesday Books Ltd: Mark J. Sachner
US Editor: Joshua Shadowens
Designer: Trudi Webb

Photo Credits: Cover, 1, 4–5, 6–7, 8–9, 10–11, 12–13, 14–15, 16, 20, 22–23, 24–25, 26–27, 28–29, 30
© Shutterstock; 17 © Ardea; 18 © Nature Picture Library; 19 © Getty Images; 21 © Barbara Dobner,
Friends of the Koala.

Library of Congress Cataloging-in-Publication Data

Owen, Ruth, 1967–
 Koalas / by Ruth Owen.
    pages cm. — (Dr. Bob's amazing world of animals)
 Includes index.
 ISBN 978-1-47779-024-3 (library) — ISBN 978-1-47779-025-0 (pbk.) —
 ISBN 978-1-47779-026-7 (6-pack)
 1. Koala—Juvenile literature. I. Title.
 QL737.M384O94 2014
 599.2'5—dc23
                                                    2013025828

Manufactured in the United States of America

CPSIA Compliance Information: Batch #BW14WM: For Further Information contact Windmill Books, New York, New York at 1-866-478-0556

Contents

The Koala

Welcome to my amazing world of animals.
Today, we are visiting gum tree forests in
Australia to find out about koalas.

Let's investigate...

Hank's
WOOF OF WISDOM!

People often call these little animals "koala bears." They are not a type of bear, though. Koalas belong to a group of animals called **marsupials**.

Koalas spend nearly all their lives high in the branches of gum trees.

Koalas eat gum tree leaves, sleep in gum trees, and raise their babies in the treetops.

Land of the Koala

A small number of koalas live in zoos around the world. Koalas only live in the wild in one place, though, and that's Australia.

Koalas live in gum tree forests in the areas marked in red on the map.

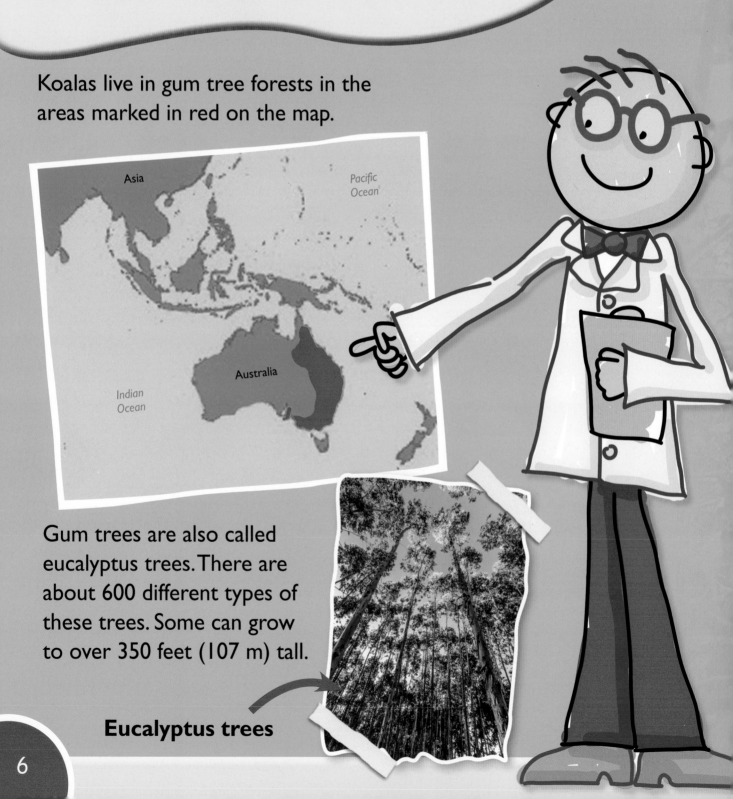

Gum trees are also called eucalyptus trees. There are about 600 different types of these trees. Some can grow to over 350 feet (107 m) tall.

Eucalyptus trees

The green or silver leaves of gum trees contain an oil that makes them smell like cough drops.

Home Ranges

A koala lives and finds its food in one area of the forest. This area is called its **home range**.

A koala's home range may be just a few trees. It might be an area several miles (km) wide.

Male koala

Adult male koalas have a body part called a scent gland on their chests. It looks like a dirty mark and releases a scent, or smell.

Scent gland

A male koala rubs his scent gland on the trees in his home range. The smell tells other males that he is around.

Hank's
WOOF OF WISDOM!

The home ranges of different koalas overlap with each other.

Koala Bodies

Koalas have thick gray or brownish-gray fur, with white fur on their chests and bellies. A koala's fur keeps it warm during cold weather. During hot weather, its thick coat protects the koala from the hot sun.

On rainy days, a koala's fur acts like a raincoat, keeping the animal dry.

Koalas have long claws for gripping branches and holding onto tree trunks.

Koala Size Chart

Weight
(adult female) =
11 to 18 pounds
(5–8 kg)

An adult koala measures about 30 inches (76 cm)
from its nose to its bottom.

Weight
(adult male) =
14 to 26 pounds
(6.5–12 kg)

What's on the Menu?

Koala's eat gum tree leaves, but not every kind. These leaf-eating animals are fussy eaters.

Even though there are hundreds of different types of gum trees, koalas only eat certain kinds.

An adult koala can eat over 1 pound (450 g) of gum tree leaves each day.

The oil in gum tree leaves is poisonous to most animals. Koalas have certain kinds of **bacteria** in their stomachs, however, that break down the poison. This allows the koalas to eat the leaves safely.

Sleepy Koalas

Koalas are mostly active at night. They climb or leap from tree to tree looking for tasty leaves.

A koala spends about four hours each day **foraging** and eating. It spends the other 20 hours asleep!

zzzzzz

Gum tree leaves contain very little **nutrition**. This means a koala's food does not give it much energy.

ZZZZzz

To save energy, a koala spends a large amount of its time resting and sleeping.

A Jelly Bean Joey

Adult koalas meet up and **mate** between August and December.

About 35 days after she mates, a female koala gives birth to a tiny baby. The baby is called a joey.

The joey climbs into a cozy **pouch** on the front of its mother's body.

The pouch is here.

All female marsupials have a pouch.

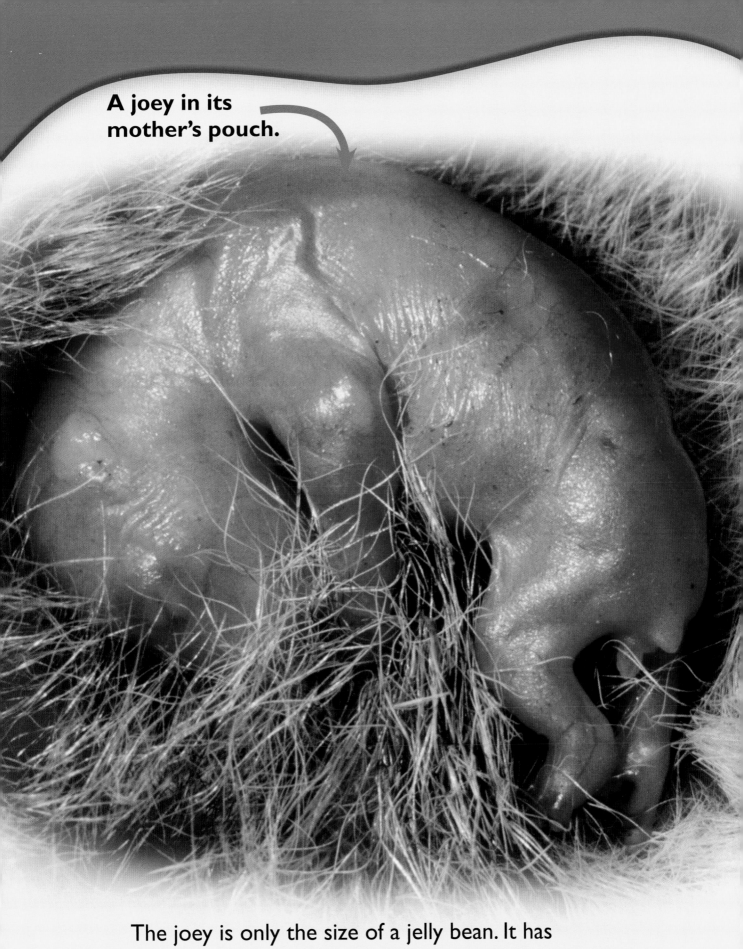

A joey in its mother's pouch.

The joey is only the size of a jelly bean. It has no ears or fur, and its tiny eyes are closed.

A Growing Joey

The tiny koala joey lives in its mother's pouch. It drinks milk from its mother's body and slowly grows bigger.

All marsupial animals are **mammals.** They give birth to tiny, live babies that are not fully formed. Marsupial babies finish growing inside their mothers' pouches.

This joey is about 12 weeks old.

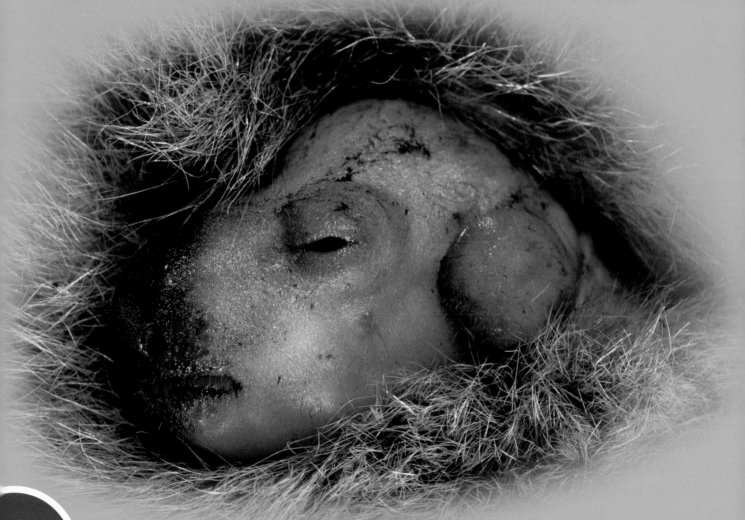

By the time the joey is six months old, its ears and fur have grown. The baby koala's eyes are open, too.

Now, the joey looks out of its mother's pouch as it rides through the treetops.

Joey

Koala Baby Food

Once the joey has grown enough to look out of the pouch, it starts to try new foods.

The joey still drinks milk, but it also eats a special runny, baby food called pap. It also snacks on leaves.

Joey

Mother koala

Joey

Pap

A mother koala's body makes pap from gum tree leaves. The pap comes out of the mother's body as waste, and the joey licks it up.

Hank's WOOF OF WISDOM!

Pap contains bacteria from a mother koala's stomach. These bacteria go into her joey's stomach. Now the joey is all set for eating poisonous gum tree leaves as it grows up.

Joey food

All Grown Up

By the time it is nine months old, a joey is too big to fit in its mother's pouch.

The joey eats leaves, but still drinks milk, too.

The big joey rides through the gum tree forest on its mother's back.

A treetop piggyback ride

A joey leaves its mother when it is about 18 months old. It is ready to live alone and find a home range of its own.

Koalas become adults when they are about four years old.

No Place to Call Home

Koalas need gum tree forests. The forests are their homes and the only places where they can find food.

Today, koalas are in danger of losing their **habitat**. People cut down gum tree forests to build houses, roads, shopping malls, and factories.

When too many koalas try to live in a small area of forest, there is not enough food for all of them.

A gum tree forest

Hank's
WOOF OF WISDOM!

If there are no gum tree forests, there will be no koalas!

Koalas in Danger!

With areas of forest getting smaller, koalas are forced to walk from place to place to find food. Once they are on the ground, they are in big danger!

As a koala walks from one patch of forest to another, it might wander onto a road. Every year, thousands of koalas are killed by cars and trucks.

Hank's
WOOF OF WISDOM!

Drivers in Australia are warned to slow down for koalas, especially at night.

Sadly, many koalas are also attacked or killed by pet dogs when they come down to the ground.

Friends of Koalas

Thankfully, many **conservation organizations** in Australia are working hard to protect and help koalas.

A carer from a koala rescue center.

These organizations try to get the government and construction companies to build in areas where there are no gum tree forests.

Koalas at a rescue center.

They help people plant gum trees on their land. This creates new areas of forest.

If a koala is injured by a car or dog, carers from koala rescue centers help the animal. They nurse the koala and hopefully release it back into the wild once it is recovered.

Glossary

bacteria (bak-TEER-ee-uh)
Tiny living things that can only be seen with a microscope. Some bacteria are helpful, while others are harmful.

conservation organizations (kon-sur-VAY-shun or-guh-nuh-ZAY-shunz)
Groups of people who do work to protect animals, plants, and wild habitats.

foraging (FOR-uj-ing)
Searching for food.

habitat (HA-buh-tat)
The place where an animal or plant normally lives. A habitat may be a forest, the ocean, or a backyard.

home range (HOHM RAYNJ)
The area where an animal lives and finds its food.

mammals (MA-mulz)
Warm-blooded animals that have a backbone and usually have hair, breathe air, and feed milk to their young.

marsupials (mar-SOO-pee-uhlz)
A group of mammals that includes koalas and kangaroos. Female marsupials raise their young in pouches on their bellies.

mate (MAYT)
When a male and a female animal get together to produce young.

nutrition (noo-TRIH-shun)
The goodness in food that gives an animal energy and keeps it healthy.

pouch (POWCH)
A pocket-like part of a female marsupial's belly that is used for carrying her young.

Dr. Bob's Fast Fact Board

Koalas get most of the water they need by eating gum tree leaves. There is a little water inside each leaf, and rainwater and dew collect on the leaves.

Koalas make a noise that sounds like a snore followed by a burp. The noise is called a bellow.

A koala lives for about 8 to 15 years.

You don't have to live in Australia to be a friend to koalas. Go online and find a conservation organization that helps koalas. The organization's website will give you lots of ideas for ways that you can help.

Websites

For web resources related to the subject of this book, go to:

www.windmillbooks.com/weblinks

and select this book's title.

Read More

Clark, Willow. *Koalas*. Up a Tree. New York: PowerKids Press, 2012.

Kawa, Katie. *Baby Koalas*. Cute and Cuddly: Baby Animals. New York: Gareth Stevens Leveled Readers, 2011.

Kras, Sarah Louise. *Koalas*. Australian Animals. Mankato, MN: Capstone Press, 2010.

Index